Aura
of
Love

Aura
of
Love

Walter Rinder

Celestial Arts
Millbrae, California

Cover & interior design by Betsy Bruno

Copyright © 1978 by Walter Rinder

CELESTIAL ARTS
231 Adrian Road
Millbrae, California 94030

First Printing, February 1978
Made in the United States of America

Library of Congress Cataloging in Publication Data

Rinder, Walter
    Aura of love.

    I. Title.
PS3568.I5A94   811'.5'4   77-90026
ISBN 0-89087-222-8

1 2 3 4 5 6 7 — 83 82 81 80 79 78

Introduction

This introduction is being written upon a white sandy beach on the southern tip of the Florida coast.

I left my home in Oregon May 5, 1977, on an extensive journey exploring the entire spectrum of my country in a camper pickup truck. By the time this book is published I will be heading back to the West Coast after a year of migrating within my country's natural beauty and within the environments of many different types of people.

There were several reasons for this particular trip but most significant was to meet as many people as I was able, especially those who had written me letters expressing their feelings toward my books. I felt the desire for a more personal contact and was truly inspired by their sensitive, honest responses.

Meeting strangers and making friends to share loving with was my hope. The seed for this book lay dormant in me for many years of my life. The human beings on this journey nurtured that seed and it grew into a need to share these feelings with you.

The missing link in building relationships of intimacy and the asserting of love was found in the loving of oneself. The closeness, the interest that was allowed to be shared by each person I met seemed to be determined by the degree of self-love or lack of it.

The nature and capacity of my loving them was uncomfortable to many people. I feel self-love, self-pride, would have given them a greater understanding and patience of who I am and the rich feelings we could have shared and our points of contact would have been stronger and more desirable.

I appreciate all the people who gave me of their time and consideration thus far on this journey of understanding. Whether we shared for a few hours, a few days or weeks, each togetherness stimulated my growth in searching for truths. Those simple, instinctive needs that lie within each one of us bringing harmony among humankind.

We are never whole unless we are sharing ourselves with someone in friendship and love. Loving oneself is the beginning.

Only those who love themselves can experience who they are and who others truly are.

This journey has illuminated that truth and I will constantly light the path of my destiny and hopefully influence others toward theirs.

Please feel free to write me of your feelings, your reactions to my poetry. We all need to express ourselves. Through the expression of others, we learn about ourselves.

Walter Rinder, c/o Celestial Arts, 231 Adrian Road, Millbrae, CA 94030

To all the lovers,
all over the world,
and to those who dream, someday!

Portland, Oregon
Walter Rinder

I love you . . .
. . . and I love myself for allowing
the freedom to flourish,
for expressing my emotions without boundaries
created by my mind.
The only way I know to be loved
is to offer my loving
as a greeting of who I am.

I have the courage to love,
and to show it.

Loving myself allows me . . .
    to constantly increase my capacity
    and to be in rhythm
with all kinds of loving relationships,
    to cherish my talents, my vitality,
    and to deal with all the feelings
given to me by my Creator.

I may say I love you
    and increase your faith,
    but when my actions follow
    and honor my words,
I will be proud of who I am.

To be a living example
    of a loving spirit
    on the physical plane
    of existence
    is my goal
and the only reward I seek.

When I do not feel guilty
        about who I am,
nor fear the secrets of my heart,
then the beautiful person
I am striving to be
can liberate my needs and desires,
so I might share more of myself
        with you and all others
        my life touches.

When I feel guilty,
then I must pretend
    to be what I am not,
    or be careful
    to offer
    only those parts you will accept.
This is such a precious waste
                of life.

The more I give of myself
the more I realize I am able to give.
Our discoveries and experiences
then become important
to be trusting and knowing
each other.

Wisdom will come
when I am consistent
and no longer feel insecure,
when I am constantly able
to give you the security
embodied in the truths
I have discovered.

Once I begin giving
I am unable to stop;
the more you accept
the more I can give.
You support me by your receiving.

As I encourage you
        to search for your own truth
        by asserting my personality,
We both will be rewarded
        by a growing relationship,
        and will desire the togetherness
        to reach its full potential,
        without seeking shelter
        from risks and chances
        or allowing the past
        to condemn our present.

I am not the whole person I appear to be.
The only time I am whole
is when I am loving someone
besides myself.
The flesh and the mind
require continuous stimulation
to develop inner order
and balance.
What better way to gain these
than by the excitement of loving you?

The shadows of your fears and doubts
can be illuminated
by the dawn of my caring.
Each morning will burst forth
a sunrise
and each evening can settle
into a glorious time
of passion or peace.

The one commitment I make to you
        is my personal honesty—
That promise is
        now and forever.
My honesty at times
        may hurt you,
causing resistance
        to my love,
though that will never
        be my intent,
but understanding can soon heal
        the hurt.

Love, too often, is only a dream,
an ideal thought to be unattainable—
a dance upon the clouds of our fantasies.
Now that we have made it real,
I can hold you in my arms and dance
to the musical accompaniment of nature,
played by the richness of the earth,
while all humanity looks on.

The struggle for any dream
is always worth the effort,
for in the struggle lies its strength,
    and fulfillment
      toward the changing seasons
    or ourselves.

Your needs become my desires;
your growth becomes my nurturing;
your happiness becomes my ecstasy.

We are a part of the same universal force,
although our shapes,
      personalities and color
may vary as the maple
      and cedar and alder trees
      grow close together,
      even in each other's shadows,
all the while keeping
their individual natures
as life commands.

As I respect myself,
bathing in my own dignity
and am kind to myself,
so too do I share
these attitudes with you.
If I am harsh, cruel,
and unkind to myself,
these attitudes also I share with you.

If I surrender to selfishness,
fulfilling only my own desires,
then I retreat from our love—
We are blown apart by the winds
                    of indifference.

Loving for me is a way of life:
Passion, affection, creativity,
    commitment and devotion
are but some of the paths I travel,
for there are many others.
I must exercise all those parts of me
    that lead toward my destiny
    and influence yours.

We can journey side by side,
but there will be situations
    in which I lead or follow,
    as with you.

The seasons always follow
their natural order:
    Winter may extend into Spring,
    Indian Summer may run into Fall,
    unfolding as nature intended.
Sometimes I am as Winter,
dormant and within my solitude,
and you are as Spring,
alive and with new growth,
but loving will always bring us
back into sharing the same season.

Only those who truly love you
can experience
    who you are.

The earth is my home
    to construct a foundation of loving.
Let us help each other
    in the building of our lives,
    as the trees give sanctuary
        to the birds,
    the flowers give life substance
        to the bees,
    the rivers and the lakes satisfy the thirst
        of the creatures,
    and the clouds replenish the waters
    and the sun brings everything together.

We are a reflection of each other.
Is not the reality of a reflection
    an image of the same?
And are not the reality and the mirrored image
    flowing together upon the waters of truth?
Look within me
    and you will see the banquet of love
    I have prepared for you.

Eyes often express
the intentions of the heart.
Let my eyes say
that we are more the same
    than is realized.
In silent interpretation
they reveal my world
and the world I hope for us.

To enter the "Spectrum of Love"
you begin by learning to love yourself.

Mark,
I wanted something to
show you how I felt about us! I
thought this said it as, if not better than
I ever could. So All I want to say
is:
I LOVE you, your
MAKE ME WHAT I
AM!
Love,
me

Then all reasons,
   all deeds,
   all forms of communication
will lead you to your infinite potential
   as a loving human being
   who attracts the force
   of loving within others.

WALT RINDER